👍 *The essentials...*

Times Square

Learn about the daily life of immigrants at Ellis Island ▶ *1*

Attend a Gospel Service in Harlem ▶ *9*

Ice Skate at Rockefeller Center ▶ *7*

Listen to a jazz concert in one of the venues in SoHo or Greenwich, or the Apollo Theater ▶ *4* and ▶ *9*

Salivate over delicacies at the shops in Chelsea Market ▶ *7*

Sip a glass of wine and watch the sunset at a rooftop bar ▶ *1*, ▶ *4* and ▶ *10*

...and our favorites...

Take the Staten Island Ferry to admire New York from another angle ▶ *1*

Picnic in Riverside Park, on the banks of the Hudson ▶ *7*

Taste Coal-fired-oven pizza at Juliana's under the Brooklyn Bridge ▶ *10*

* The numbers indicate the sections.

Rooftop bar

© Mlenny/iStockphoto.com

© Maurizio Rellini/Sime/Photononstop

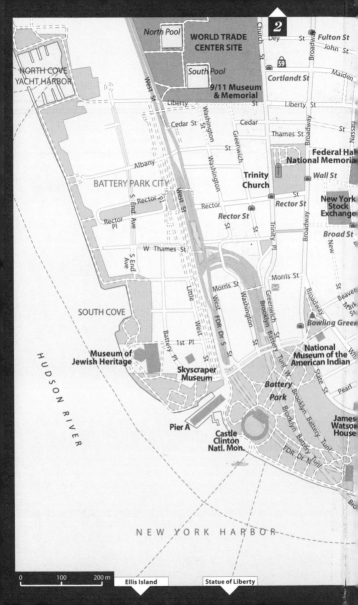

HUDSON RIVER

NORTH COVE
YACHT HARBOR

North Pool

WORLD TRADE
CENTER SITE

South Pool

9/11 Museum
& Memorial

Church St

Dey St

Fulton St

John St

Broadway

Maiden

Cortlandt St

Liberty St

Cedar St

Thames St

Federal Hall
National Memoria

Wall St

New York
Stock
Exchange

Broad St

New St

Beaver

Mark

Bowling Green

National
Museum of the
American Indian

State St

Pearl St

James
Watson
House

DESBR...

Liberty St

West St

Cedar St

Washington St

Greenwich St

Trinity
Church

Albany

Rector St

BATTERY PARK CITY

Rector Pl

S End Ave

Rector Pl

W Thames St

S End Ave

Little West St

Morris St

West St

FDR Dr S St

Washington St

Greenwich St

Brooklyn Battery Tunl

Morris St

Rector St

Rector St

Trinity Pl

Broadway

SOUTH COVE

Battery Pl

1st Pl

Museum of
Jewish Heritage

Skyscraper
Museum

Battery Pl

Battery
Park

Brooklyn Battery Tunl W

Brooklyn Battery Tunl

Pier A

Castle
Clinton
Natl. Mon.

FDR Dr N

Bro

NEW YORK HARBOR

0   100   200 m

Ellis Island

Statue of Liberty

East River

Fulton St

Fulton St

77 Fulton St

98 46

99

79

Beekman

Front St

FDR Dr S

John St

Cliff St

Pearl St

South Street
Seaport
Museum

Platt St

Gold St

Maiden Ln

PIER 17

Federal
Reserve
Bank

Liberty St

Water St

John St

South St

PIER 16

Cedar St

Pearl St

SOUTH STREET SEAPORT
HISTORIC DISTRICT

St

Pine St

FDR Dr N

PIER 14

Wall St

**Museum of
American Finance**

Water St

Front St

Wall St

South St

FDR Dr S

PIER 13

Wall St

FINANCIAL
DISTRICT

Beaver St

William St

Pearl St

Front St

South St

FDR Dr N

PIER 11

Old Slip

IKEA Ferry/
East River Ferry

Broad St

William St

1

28

Stone St

**Fraunces
Tavern
Museum**

Pearl St

Broad St

South St

FDR Dr S

PORT AUTHORITY
DOWNTOWN HELIPORT

East River

*Whitehall St-
South Ferry*

FDR Dr N

PIER 6

State St

Whitehall St

FDR Dr S

**Battery
Maritime
Building**

South Ferry

George St

**Staten
Island Ferry
Terminal**

Brooklyn Battery Tunl W

Battery Tunl E

V

falafel and other Middle Eastern fare. To get seats, avoid the lunch rush.

TAKE A BREAK

Chinatown Ice Cream Factory – *65 Bayard St.* - Ⓜ *Canal St.* Serving ice cream in unexpected flavors like Thai iced tea and, this shop makes for a tasty black sesame break in the heart of Chinatown.

Barnes & Noble – *270 Greenwich St.* - Ⓜ *Chambers St.* Take refuge in this bookstore in inclement weather and browse thousands of books, including a number in languages other than English. The children's area is welcoming and has regular readings. Free WiFi throughout.

SHOPPING

Head east along **Canal Street** (Ⓜ Canal St.) if you're a fan of shopping for bargains. You'll find T-shirts, bags watches and more. Haggle over the prices, but beware of counterfeits.

Canal Street Market – *265 Canal St.* – Ⓜ *Chambers St.* Inviting indoor market with a dozen-odd stands selling trendy home goods and accessories from local designers. There are a few food vendors here but little seating, and you'd do much better to go to a nearby restaurant.

Century 21 – *22 Cortlandt St.* - Ⓜ *Cortland St.* A huge store dedicated to discounting main US and European brands. There are real bargains to be had here.

Downtown Music Gallery – *13 Monroe St.* - Ⓜ *East Broadway - 12h-18h.* A specialised selection of CDs and vinyl records curated by passionate music collectors.

Philip Williams Posters – *122 Chambers St.* – Ⓜ *Chambers St.* Try this shop for vintage posters and prints featuring movie stars and famous advertising imagery.

The Mysterious Bookshop – *35 Warren St.* - Ⓜ *Chambers St.* Delightful shop stocking more than 10,000 mystery and crime books, new, used, and collectible.

NIGHTLIFE

Macao Trading Co. - *311 Church St.* - Ⓜ *Canal St.* Set in a former opium bar, this lounge serves inventive and well-prepared cocktails.

Smith & Mills – *71 North Moore St.* - Ⓜ *Franklin St.* One of our favorite places in Tribeca: a small retro bar seemingly out of a movie set with great cocktails and reasonable prices. *(dishes $13-25).*

Terroir *24 Harrison St.* - Ⓜ *Franklin St.* Happy hour from 16h, several dozen wines by the glass, and toothsome bar snacks make this a welcome afternoon pit-stop. *(dishes $10-17).*

Addresses described in section 1:
146 77 79 98 99

Just north of the World Trade Center site, Tribeca's streets are lined in chic restaurants, art galleries and warehouses-turned-lofts. To the east, Chinatown is crowded and colorful, where gadget-filled stalls alternate with tea merchants and restaurants whose aromas pique the senses.

Woolworth Building

VISIT

Harrison Street – M *Franklin St.* A row of Federal-style houses (nos 25-41), built between 1796 and 1828, gives an idea of the Tribeca of that era.

White Street – M *Canal St.* Good example of high-end urban architectural design and craftsmanship of the 19C, typical of Tribeca, with its brick façades in several colors or cast-iron columns.

AT&T Building – *Walker St., at the corner of Avenue of the Americas (6th Ave.) - M Franklin St., Canal St.* The lobby of this highly regarded 1918 Art Deco building is decorated with splendid mosaics.

Chinatown★★ – M *Canal St.* Known in the late 19C for its brothels, gaming rooms and opium dens, Chinatown today is chaotic but colorful. Walk bustling streets **Canal, Mott and Mulberry** before taking a break in **Columbus Park**, where elderly locals play mahjong.

Museum of Chinese in America – *215 Centre St. - M Canal St. - www.mocanyc.org - Tue-Wed, Fri-Sun 11h-18h (Thu 11h-21h, free first Thu) - $10.* This museum explores the lives and experiences of Chinese communities in America.

WHERE TO EAT

WHERE TO ENJOY A PICNIC?
City Hall Park★ (M City Hall) is the choice of area office workers. Snack on Chinese takeaway, purchased on Mott Street and East Broadway, in **Columbus Park** (M Canal St.) or enjoy **Washington Market Park** (M Chambers St.).

24 **Fuleen Seafood** – *11 Division St. - M Canal St., Grand St. - ✆ 212 941 6888 - www.fuleenrestaurant.com - open until 4h in the morning - lunch menu $6.* The value for money at this Cantonese eatery can't be beat.

35 **Nom Wah Tea Parlor** – *13 Doyers St. - M E. Broadway. - ✆ 212 962 6047 - nomwah.com - dishes $4-7.* Operating since 1920. Come for reasonably priced *dim sum* and tea in delightfully retro surrounds.

51 **Peking Duck House** – *28 Mott St. - M Canal St. - ✆ 212 227 1810 - www.pekingduckhousenyc.com - dishes $13-75.* The glazed house duck ($56) is a delight not to be missed.

56 **Nish Nush** – *88 Reade St. - M Chambers St. - ✆ 212 964 1318 - www.nishnushnyc.com - dishes $7-14.* Fragrant

City Hall Park

Broadway

Grand St

Elizabeth

Grand St

Eldridge

Allen

Orchard

Crosby

Mott

Bowery

Chrystie

SARA D. ROOSEVELT PARK

Hester St

Hester St

Street

Museum of Chinese in America

Centre

Mulberry

St

LITTLE ITALY

Canal St

Canal

COLONNADE

Forsyth

Canal St

Canal St

Lafayette

83

Canal St

Canal St

Manhattan

Manhattan

Pike

Eldridge Street Synagogue

Street

Private Danny Chen Way

St

Mott

Confucius Plaza

Bowery

Manhattan Brg

Street

Baxter

St

61

CHINATOWN

8

Franklin

Lafayette

St

35

51

Division St

Market

24

N

S

Street

Centre

Columbus Park

Doyers St

Street

E. Broadway

Street

Madison

Hogan Pl

Chatham Square

Henry

Street

Broadway

Worth St

FOLEY SQUARE

Worth St

Worth St

James Pl

Madison St

Catherine

Monroe

62

Street

Lafayette

Pearl

Cardinal Hayes Pl

Park Row

Pearl

CIVIC CENTER

Reade St

Chambers St

Municipal Building

James St

Madison St

Catherine

St

Cherry

Chambers St

Centre

Park Row

Catherine

Slip

Slip

City Hall

Av. of the Finest

FDR Dr S

City Hall

Brooklyn Bridge-City Hall

Brooklyn Brg

City Hall Park

Frankfort St

Robert F. Wagner Sr Pl.

Pearl St

South St

Row

Spruce St

Frankfort St

Brooklyn Brg

Gold

Dover

Park

Beekman

Tour Gehry

St

LOWER MANHATTAN

Water St

Peck Slip

FDR Dr S

BROOKLYN BRIDGE

Theatre Aly

Ann

Fulton St

Broadway-Nassau

Nassau

William

Fulton St

77

Fulton St

Cliff St

Pearl

Beekman

98

46

99

South St

79

East River

Fulton St

John St

John St

John St

Gold

Platt

South Street Seaport Museum

Water St

FDR Dr N

PIER

Federal Reserve Bank

Maiden Ln

Liberty St

Cedar

Pine

Maiden Ln

SOUTH STREET SEAPORT HISTORIC DISTRICT

John St

PIER 16

deral Hall Memorial

E 4th St
Great Jones St
Bond St
Bleecker St
NOHO
2 Ave
E 3rd St
E 2nd St
E Houston St
E 1st St
E Houston St
Lafayette St
Mott St
Bowery
Chrystie St
Forsyth St
SARA D.
Eldridge St
Allen St
Orchard St
Ludlow St
Essex St
Norfolk St
Suffolk St
Clinton St
Star
Rivi
EAST VILLAGE
E 4th St
E 3rd St
E 2nd St
E Houston St
62
92
80
Rivington
65
65

Old Saint Patrick's Cathedral
14
71
Prince
New Museum of Contemporary Art
23
Stanton
29
Delancey St
Essex St
Delancey St
W

NOLITA
Spring St
36
Elizabeth St
Bowery
77
Delancey St
Lower East Side Tenement Museum
15
Broome St
Clinton
13
Kenmare
St
Bowery
Bowery
Chrystie St
FORSYTH St
ROOSEVELT
Allen St
11
Norfolk St
Suffolk
31
BOWERY
Broome
Street
Eldridge St
Street
LOWER EAST SIDE
Centre Market Pl
Grand St
Street
Grand St
Grand
Eldridge St
Allen St
Essex St
Seward Park
Museum of Chinese in America
Hester St
LITTLE ITALY
Mulberry St
Elizabeth St
St
PARK
Eldridge St
Street
Street
Canal
E Broadway
E Broadway
Henry St
Madison
Eldridge Street Synagogue
Division St
Pike
Canal
Centre St
Canal St
Mulberry
Mott St
Canal
St
COLONNADE
Confucius Plaza
Manhattan Brg
Manhattan Brg N
CHINATOWN
Bayard St
61
8
Pell St
35
Bowery
51
24
Division St
Market St
Henry St
Cherry St
Manhattan Brg
Leonard
Hogan Pl
Columbus Park
St
Baxter St
Chatham Sq
Chatham
St
St
Henry St
Monroe St
62
COLEMAN PARK

FOLEY SQUARE
Worth St
Worth St
Row
Pl
Catherine St
Catherine Slip
Cherry St
Market Slip
South St
CIVIC CENTER
Pearl St
Cardinal Hayes Pl
James St
Madison St
Water St
FDR Dr N
Chambers St
Municipal Building

0   125   250 m

Russ & Daughters

restaurant serving rustic specialties, such as terrine of wild boar or river trout, to elegant clientèle.

[29] Russ & Daughters Cafe – 127 Orchard St. - **M** Delancey St, Essex St.. - ✆ 212 475 4880 ext. 2 ext 2 - www.russanddaughterscafe.com.com - most dishes $8-20. The cafe outpost of the popular shop nearby serves up Jewish comfort food, including latkes (fried potato pancakes), bagels, and a towering pastrami sandwich.

[51] La Esquina – 106 Kenmare St. - **M** Spring St. - ✆ 646 613 7100 - www.esquinanyc.com. Dig into gourmet Mexican fare served in 3 areas: a taqueria with reasonable prices (quesadillas $6-8), a café (dishes $10-17) and an upscale restaurant (reservations at least 3 weeks in advance, dishes $24-32).

[36] Lovely Day – 96 Elizabeth St. - **M** Bowery - ✆ 212 925 3310 - http://lovelydaynyc.com - dishes around $10. With its floral wallpaper and red moleskin benches, you'd never guess this spot serves delicious Thai dishes!

[44] Mottsu – 285 Mott St. - **M** Broadway-Lafayette St. - ✆ 212 343 8017 - www.mottsu.com - dishes $10-24. Very good Japanese cuisine including Maki, sushi and fish dishes.

TAKE A BREAK

[8] Dudley's – 85 Orchard St. - **M** Delancey St. Nice decor, with large mirrors, wooden floors and marble

tables, where you can try cocktails, beer and wine, to a jazzy background soundtrack.

[13] Eileen's Cheesecake – 17 Cleveland Pl. - **M** Spring St. The best cheesecake in New York!

[15] Il Laboratorio del Gelato – 95 Orchard St. - **M** Delancey St. Rich, creamy gelato in a small shop directly overlooking the "laboratory". Don't hesitate to sample their original flavors.

SHOPPING

The Lower East Side focuses on designer boutiques, thrift stores and antique shops.

Luxury thrift store **Ina [71]** (21 Prince St., **M** Spring St.) has a good selection of designer womenswear.

[65] Economy Candy – 108 Rivington St.- **M** Essex St. Entire shelves of bulk sweets, imported candy bars and dried fruits, with or without sugar!

[60] Self Edge – **M** Delancey St., Essex St. Ultra-cool, ultra-pricey Japanese men's denim.

NIGHTLIFE

[77] Bowery Ballroom – 6 Delancey St. - **M** Bowery - www.boweryballroom.com. One of the best New York concert halls, hosting well-known rock bands and newcomers.

[92] The Slipper Room – 167 Orchard St. - **M** Essex St. - www.theslipperroom.com. Grab a seat for burlesque numbers, contortionists, puppets, tap dancers, and comedians. Ages 21+.

Addresses described in section 2:
[24] [51] [8] [62]

Once known for its population of Italians, today the insular Neopolitan village of Little Italy consists of just a few stores and trattorias. For a Sunday stroll, try the Lower East Side (LES) instead—you can shop on Orchard Street while enjoying an authentic New York bagel.

Lower East Side Tenement Museum

VISIT

Little Italy – Ⓜ *Canal St., Spring St.* The first Italian immigrants came together in this neighborhood, which soon became the haunt of the Mafia. Today, the streets have recovered some serenity. **Mulberry Street** is heady with the aroma of tasty Italian dishes.

Henry Street – Ⓜ *East Broadway.* This street was the center of the first Jewish neighborhood. It has some interesting architecture of the late 19C. Founded in 1893, the Henry Street Settlement (No. 263) was a kind of social center, providing care, financial assistance and social services for poor people.

Eldridge Street Synagogue★ – *12 Eldridge St.* - Ⓜ *East Broadway - 10h-17h (Fri 15h) - closed Sat and Jewish holidays - $12.* New York's first synagogue founded by Jews of Eastern Europe (1887) boasts an eclectic façade that skillfully blends Romanesque Revival, Gothic and pseudo-Moorish styles.

Orchard Street – Ⓜ *Delancey St.- Essex St.* The southern part of Orchard Street is occupied by cheap clothing and luggage stores; to the north are chic boutiques and restaurants. Every Sunday there is a lively open-air market (*from 10h*).

Lower East Side Tenement Museum★★ – *108 Orchard St.* - Ⓜ *Delancey St. - www.tenement.org - guided visit 10h-18h30 - $25 - reservation advised.* Exploring the housing conditions of immigrant families, this museum uses personal objects and documents to tell their stories.

Ludlow Street★ – Ⓜ *Delancey St. - Essex St.* With its cafés and shops, these blocks parallel to Orchard Street offer an agreeable stroll.

Nolita – Ⓜ *2 Ave., Bowery.* Cafés, small restaurants and trendy boutiques dot the northern part of Little Italy (NoLIta stands for "North of Little Italy"), although it does not have the elegance of SoHo or Chelsea.

New Museum of Contemporary Art★ – *235 Bowery* - Ⓜ *Bowery - www.newmuseum.org - Wed-Sun 11h-18h (Thu 21h, pay-as-you-wish from 19h)- $18.* This museum houses collections oriented towards new media, digital pop art and installations.

Saint Patrick's Old Cathedral – Ⓜ *Spring St.* Built in Gothic Revival style (1815), this was, until 1879, the Catholic cathedral of New York.

WHERE TO EAT

☺ **WHERE TO PICNIC?** Sit around the fountain in **Seward Park** on East Broadway (Ⓜ East Broadway), and enjoy a pastrami sandwich bought at a delicatessen on the corner.

🍴 **Freemans** - *191 Chrystie St.* - Ⓜ *Bowery, 2 Ave.* - ✆ *212 420 0012 - www.freemansrestaurant.com - dishes $12-20 (lunch), $20-30 (evening).* A hip

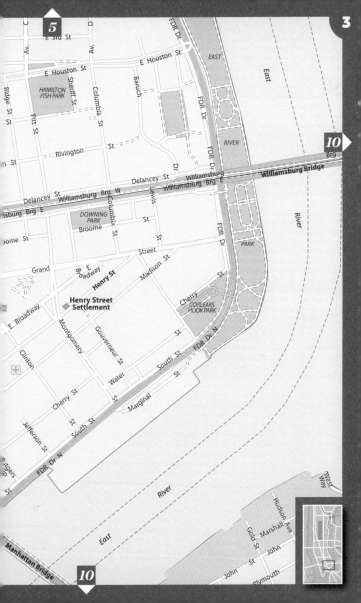

E 3rd St

E Houston St

E Houston St

EAST

East

HAMILTON
FISH PARK

Sheriff St

Columbia St

Baruch St

FDR Dr

Ridge St

Pitt St

RIVER

Rivington St

Delancey St

Williamsburg Br

Williamsburg Bridge

Brg

10

Delancey St

Williamsburg Brg W

Williamsburg Brg

River

sburg Brg E

Columbia St

Lewis St

DOWNING
PARK

Broome

St

PARK

Dome St

Street

Grand

Broadway E

Madison St

Henry St

Cherry

St

Henry Street
Settlement

CORLEARS
HOOK PARK

E Broadway

Montgomery St

Gouverneur St

St

Clinton St

Water St

South St

FDR Dr N

Cherry St

Marginal

Jefferson St

South St

utgers

FDR Dr N

West
Way

ip St

River

Manhattan Bridge

East

Hudson Ave

Gold St

Marshall St

John St

John

St

10

Plymouth

Chelsea Piers

W 19th St

High Line

W 18th St
W 17th St
W 16th St
11th Ave
W 15th St

Chelsea Market

10th Ave

W 15th St
W 14th St

9 Ave

MEATPACKING DISTRICT

13th St

W 18th St
W 17th St
W 16th St
W 15th St

8th Ave

W 19th St

W 19th Ave

18 St

64

W 16th St

7th

8 Ave

14 St

W 14th St
W 14th

14 St

Greenwich Ave

7th Ave

W 12th S

91

Little West 12th St

Gansevoort St

Hudson St

10

W 12th St

West

W 11th St

97

Bloomfield St

Whitney Museum
of American Art

Horatio

Jane St

W 12th St

Greenwich St

8th Ave

Bank

St

Perry St

Charles St

37

4th

W 10th

76

Bethune

Bank

Washington St

W 11th St

Hudson St

22

Greenwich St

Bleecker

Christopher St
Sheridan Sq

Charles Ln

HISTORIC
GREENWICH VILLAGE

West St

Christopher St

Barrow

Morto

HUDSON RIVER

GREENWICH VILLAGE

Washington St

Greenwich St

St. Luke's Pl

HUDSON
PARK

Clarkson

W Houston St

Washington St

Hudson St

King St

Charlton

Vanda

PIER 40

West St

Holland Tu

PIER 34

West St

St Canal

Holland Tunl E

0   125   250 m

2

Watts

6

2

WHERE TO EAT

⊛ WHERE TO HAVE A PICNIC?
Chelsea Market (✦ Visits) is perfect for snacks to be enjoyed on the piers, now part of a riverfront park, along the Hudson.

10 Corner Bistro – 331, West 4th St. - **M** 8 Ave. - ✆ 212 242 9502 - open until 2h and 3h - dishes $8-10. The burgers served here are among the best in the city and come at a reasonable price!

12 Dean & Deluca – 560 Broadway - **M** Prince St. - ✆ 212 226 6800 - www.deandeluca.com - allow $10-20. The stalls of this market overflow with fine groceries, fresh salads and tasty prepared foods, on site or takeaway (no seating).

22 Frankies – 570 Hudson St. - **M** Christopher St. - ✆ 212 924 0818 - www.frankiesspuntino.com - dishes $11-26. Crostini, grilled pork and squid are favorites at this trattoria that opts for simplicity and good products.

57 Mary's Fish Camp – 64 Charles St. - **M** Christopher St. - ✆ 646 486 2185 - www.marysfishcamp.com - closed Sun - dishes $15-28. With a noisy but friendly vibe, this eatery celebrates the seafood of the east coast.

60 Mooncake Foods – 28 Watts St. - **M** Canal St. (1) - ✆ 212 219 8888 - mooncakefoods.com. Pint-size cheerful Asian-fusion eatery serving focusing on healthy ingredients and serving *bahn mi*, soup, salad, and small dishes. ($6-13)

TAKE A BREAK

25 Murray's Cheese Bar – 264 Bleecker St. - **M** West 4th St. From 16h onward, this cheese emporium slings beer, wine and cider and cheesy bar bites. Most ingredients are from local purveyors.

20 Housing Works – 130 Crosby St. - **M** Prince St., Broadway-Lafayette St. This non-profit bookstore and cafe support the fight against AIDS and homelessness. Sip coffee, tea, or beer and munch on baked goods from local non-profit Sweet Generation or sandwiches, salads, and soup.

SHOPPING

69 INA – 101 Thompson St. - **M** Spring St. A luxury thrift store stocking the victims of changes in fashion.

78 MoMA Design Store – 81 Spring St. - **M** Spring St. Objects and gadgets inspired by the museum's collections.

NIGHTLIFE

76 Fat Cat – 75 Christopher St. - **M** Christopher St. - fatcatmusic.org. Nightly live music plus billiards, ping pong, shuffle board, foosball, and board games are a winning combination.

79 Café Wha? – 115 McDougal St. - **M** West 4th St. - www.cafewha.com. A relic of the folkie '60s, this café is renowned for music and atmosphere.

91 Top of the Standard – 848 Washington St. - **M** 8 Ave. The bar of The Standard hotel is one of the most popular in New York. Enjoy a drink at sunset on a terrace with magnificent views.

97 Village Vanguard – 178 7th Ave. - **M** 14 St. - reservations. ✆ 212 255 4037 - www.villagevanguard.com. One of the legendary New York jazz clubs.

Addresses in neighboring sections:

121 151 156 141 15 ▶ 3

70 71 80 77 92

164 10 18 21 22 73 83 84 ▶ 5

SoHo and Greenwich Village combine a BoHo-chic atmosphere with the most beautiful masonry and cast-iron architecture anywhere in the country; NoHo in contrast reveals a funky vibe through its thrift stores and colorful disorder.

Meatpacking District from the High Line

VISIT

West Broadway – Ⓜ *Canal St.* Contemporary art and luxury boutiques occupy West Broadway. **OK Harris Works of Art Gallery** (*No. 383*) is one of the oldest in SoHo.

Greene Street★ – Ⓜ *Prince St.* This street is flanked by an amazing collection of cast iron façades. The two most interesting, designed in 1872 in Second Empire style, are nicknamed the **King and Queen of Greene Street** (*Nos. 72-76 and 28-30*).

Broome Street – Ⓜ *Spring St.* The street contains several elegant structures, such as the Gunther Building (*Nos. 469-475*), a beautiful 1873-creation in cast iron.

Prince Street – Ⓜ *Prince St.* Boutiques, shops and art galleries line this busy street.

Broadway – Ⓜ *Prince St.* In this part of the city, Broadway is not the stronghold of theaters, but of commerce. At nos. 561-563, the **Little Singer Building** (1903) sports a typical Beaux-Arts style, with delicate floral motifs. Further on is the 1857 **E. V. Haughwout Building★** (*Nos. 488-492*), which resembles a Venetian palace and was the first building in the city with a cast iron façade and the first equipped with an elevator, installed by E.G. Otis.

Washington Square★ – Ⓜ *West 4th St.* Close to New York University, this square's plazas and green spaces are a popular leisure area and picnic spot for New Yorkers.

Historic Greenwich Village★★ – Ⓜ *West 4th St.* To the west of 6th Avenue is the oldest part of Greenwich Village, a literary and artistic center of New York in the early 1900s that has retained pretty houses of red brick or brownstone typical of the early 20C.

Meatpacking District★ – Ⓜ *8 Ave.* North of Greenwich, this former slaughterhouse district is now a trendy zone where nightclub impresarios and fashion designers have invested in the cobbled streets and vast warehouses.

High Line★★ – *From Gansevoort St. to 34th St.* Parallel to the Hudson, this elevated railway was transformed into a beautiful pedestrian promenade that starts at the Meatpacking District and winds through the Chelsea neighborhood.

Whitney Museum of American Art★★ – *99 Gansevoort St.* - Ⓜ *8 Ave.-14 St.* - www.whitney.org - daily except Tue - 10h30-18h (Thu-Sat 10h30-22h). Recently installed in a building by Renzo Piano at the edge of the Hudson, this museum of 20th and 21st century American art houses more than 10,000 works—including many by Edward Hopper—displayed in rotation. Two floors are reserved for temporary exhibitions.

Chelsea Market★ – *75, 9th Ave.* - Ⓜ *8 Ave.-14 St.* - Mon-Sat 7h-21h, Sun 8h-20h. The old Nabisco cookies factory (1898) has been converted into an appetizing gourmet market.

Rubin Museum of Art

W 18th St
W 17th St
W 16th St
UNION SQUARE
W 15th St
14 St
6 Ave
W 14th St
W 13th St
W 12th St
W 11th St
W 10th St
Jefferson Market Library
Church of the Ascension
W 9th St
Waverly
GREENWICH AND WEST VILLAGES
Washington Square Park
New York University
W 4th St
W 3rd St
Bleecker St
Houston St
Prince
Spring St
New York City Fire Museum
Dahesh Museum of Art
SOHO
Dominick St
Broome
Canal

6th Ave
5th Ave
University Pl

E 18th St
W 18th St
E 18th St
W 17th St
E 17th St
16th St
W 16th St
E 16th St
STUYVESANT SQUARE
Union Square Park
Union Square
W 15th St
E 15th St
E 14th St
3 Ave
Union Square
E 13th St
E 12th St
St Mark's-in-the-Bowery
E 11th St
Renwick Triangle
E 10th St
Stuyvesant St
Astor Pl
Cooper Union Foundation Building
8 St-NYU
St Mark's Pl.
9th
7th St
Astor Pl.
6th St
Cooper Union 41
Colonnade Row
Merchant's House Museum
E 4th St
E 4th St
Great Jones St
3rd St
Bond St
Bleecker St
NOHO
Broadway-Lafayette St
E Houston St
SARA D ROO
Prince St
Old Saint Patrick's Cathedral
Stanton St
Little Singer Building
New Museum of Contemporary Art
NOLITA
Spring St
BOWERY
E. V. Haughwout Building
Kenmare
Gunther Building
Museum of Chinese in America
LIT

Broadway
4th Ave
Lafayette St
Bowery
2nd Ave
3rd Ave
Mott St
Mulberry St
Elizabeth St
Chrystie St
Crosby St

5

5

3

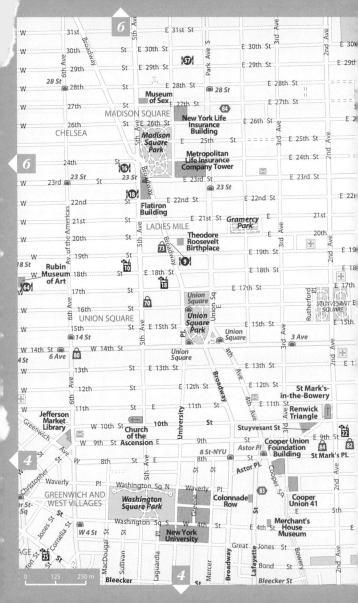

W 31st

Broadway

5th Ave

E 31st St

Park Ave S

E 30th St

3rd Ave

2nd Ave

E 30

W 30th St E 30th St E 29th St

W 29th St 6th Ave E 29th St [57] E 29th St

W 28th St 28 St E 28th St 28 St E 28th St

Museum of Sex

W 27th E 27th St E 27th St E 27th St

MADISON SQUARE

W 26th New York Life Insurance Building E 26th St 84 E 26

CHELSEA 26th 5th Ave E 25th St

Madison Square Park 25th Metropolitan Life Insurance Company Tower E 24th St E 24th St

6

W 24th 23 St 16 23 St E 23rd St 23 St E 23rd St

W 23rd Broadway E 23rd St

W 22nd 18 St E 22nd St E 22

Flatiron Building

W 21st E 21st St Gramercy Park 21st

LADIES MILE

W 20th 5th Ave Theodore Roosevelt Birthplace 20th 3rd Ave E 19

W 19th 73 Broadway E 19th St E 19th St

18 St W Rubin Museum of Art 9 E 18th St E 18

64 W 17th 17th 10 18 St E 18th St E 17

70 W 16th Union Square E 17th St Rutherford Pl STUYVESANT E 17th St

UNION SQUARE W 15th E 15th St Union Square Park Union Sq 3rd Ave E 15th St

5th Pl 3 Ave

W 14th St 14 St 80 W 14th St Union Sq Union Square 4th Ave E 1

S 6 Ave

W 13th St 6th Ave E 13th St E 13th St E 13th St

W 12th St E 12th St E 12th St St Mark's-in-the-Bowery

W 11th 11th St E 11th St Renwick Triangle

Jefferson Market Library 10th St Stuyvesant St Cooper Union Foundation Building E 9th St 22

Greenwich W 10th Church of the Ascension University 9th 84 82

W 9th E Astor Pl 8 St-NYU Astor Pl St Mark's Pl

4 W 8th 8th St St St Cooper Sq 2nd Ave

Christopher St Waverly Astor Pl 83 Cooper Union 41 5th

Waverly Pl Washington Sq N Waverly Pl Colonnade Row

GREENWICH AND WEST VILLAGES Washington Square Park Greene 5th

er St-Sq Washington Sq E 4th St Merchant's House Museum

Jones St W 4 St 25 New York University Great Jones Lafayette Bowery

MacDougal Sullivan Laguardia Mercer Broadway Bond St

0 125 250 m Bleecker Bleecker St

WHERE TO EAT

16 Eataly – *200, 5th Ave.* - M *23 St.* - 📞 *212 229 2560* - *www.eataly.com* - *dishes $10-20.* A temple to Italian gastronomy, this massive hall contains a deli, a butcher, fishmonger, bakery, a pastry shop and themed restaurants.

18 Eisenberg's – *174, 5th Ave.* - M *23 St.* - 📞 *212 675 5096* - *www. eisenbergsnyc.com* - *closed Sat and Sun eve* - *sandwiches $5-12.* One of the best old-school delis in the city.

32 La Palapa – *77 St. Mark's Pl.* - M *Astor Pl.* - 📞 *212 777 2537* - *www. lapalapa.com* - *dishes about $20.* A good spot for classic Mexican dishes like cactus salad, quesadillas and tacos.

43 Momofuku Noodle Bar – *171, 1st Ave.* - M *1st Ave.* - 📞 *212 777 7773* - *http://momofuku.com* - *dishes $8-20.* Inventive, seasonal fare including ramen and other Asian-inspired dishes.

57 Marta – *Inside Redbury Hotel, 29 East 29th St* - M *28 St.* - 📞 *212 889 6600* - *www.martamanhattan.com* - *pizza from $19.* Heavenly thin-crust pizza and antipasto platters.

64 The Café Serai – *In the Rubin Museum of Art - 150 West 17th St.* - M *18 St.* - 📞 *212 620 5000* - *www.rubinmuseum.org/ serai* - *dishes $10-16.* Sandwiches, salads and Indian-inspired dishes are on the menu at this museum café.

TAKE A BREAK

10 City Bakery – *3 West 18th St.* - M *Union Sq.* A neighborhood institution—the hot chocolate with homemade marshmallows is a must.

18 Lillie's – *13 East 17th St.* - M *Union Sq.* With its marble countertop, wood paneling and imposing chandeliers, this bar exudes Victorian elegance, even if the music is contemporary.

St Mark's Place

21 Max Brenner – *841 Broadway* - M *Union Sq.* With milkshakes, fondues waffles and more, the menu is almost exclusively dedicated to chocolate!

22 Mudspot – *307 East 9th St.* - M *Astor Pl.* Open morning, noon and night, this little cafe with garden is perfect for a snack, coffee or brunch.

33 Ten Degrees – *121 St. Marks Pl.* - M *1st Ave.* At this hip wine and cocktail bar you can nosh on charcuterie and cheese between 12h and 20h. When you buy one drink, you get one free.

SHOPPING

73 Fishs Eddy – *889 Broadway.* - M *Union Sq.* Dishware, glasses, and flatware in quirky-cool prints.

82 Cobblestones – *314 East 9th St.* - M *Astor Pl.* Heaps of vintage womens- wear fill this popular shop.

NIGHTLIFE

83 Joe's Pub – *425 Lafayette St.* - M *Astor Pl.* - *www.joespub.com.* Norah Jones and Jamie Cullum are among the stars who have played this cabaret-cum-concert room.

84 Sake Decibel – *240 East 9th St* - M *Astor Pl.* - *www.sakebardecibel.com.* NYC's original sake bar, slinging top pours since 1993.

Addresses described in section 4:
25 **76** **79**

© B. Gardel /hemis.fr

With its thrift stores, shop windows and colorful tattoo parlors, the East Village has been a mecca for both hippies and punks, a place with Gothic leanings, even if these days Bohos have replaced beatniks. In the north, Madison Square focuses on parks and cast iron buildings, such as the legendary Flatiron.

Flatiron Building

VISIT

Merchant's House Museum★ – *29 East 4th St. - Ⓜ Astor Pl. - www. merchantshouse.org - 12h-17h, Thu 12h-18h - closed Tue-Wed - $15.* This pretty brick house reflects the lifestyle of a wealthy merchant and his family in the 19C.

Cooper Union Foundation Building★ – *30 Cooper Square - Ⓜ Astor Pl.* Built in 1859, this Romanesque Revival building was the first in the United States to use steel beams.

St Mark's Place★ – *Ⓜ Astor Pl.* Shops and stalls for hippies and punks, tattoo parlors and trendy cafés are all clues to the anarchist past of this lively thoroughfare.

Tompkins Square Park★ – *Ⓜ 1st Ave.* This park has served as a rallying point over the years from socialists of the early 20C to opponents of the Vietnam War.

St Mark's-in-the-Bowery – *31 East 10th St. - Ⓜ Astor Pl.* A Greek Revival style church dating from 1799.

Renwick Triangle★ – *Ⓜ Astor Pl.* At the corner of 10th St. and Stuyvesant St. stands a set of 16 houses in brick and brownstone, designed by James Renwick (19C).

Union Square Park – *Ⓜ Union Sq.* A place to unwind, enlivened by New York's preeminent farmer's market (*Mon, Wed, Fri and Sat*), which focuses on local and organic products.

Rubin Museum of Art★★ – *150 West 17th St. - Ⓜ 18 St - 11h-17h (Wed 21h, Fri 22h (free from 18h), Sat-Sun 18h) - closed Tue - $15.* Dedicated to Tibetan, Nepalese and Bhutanese art, this museum brings together more than two millennia of culture.

Gramercy Park★ – *Ⓜ 23 St.* Surrounded by stunning homes but reserved for residents, this is one of the most beautiful parks in New York.

Theodore Roosevelt Birthplace – *28 East 20th St. - Ⓜ 23 St - www.nps.gov - Tue-Sat 9h-17h.* Closed through 2016. In this 1920 house contains a collection of objects that belonged to the 26th President of the United States and his family.

Flatiron Building★★ – *175 5th Ave. - Ⓜ 23 St.* New York's first skyscraper (1902) and at the time the tallest building in the world (307ft), this triangular 22-story steel-framed landmark in the Italianate Beaux-Arts style was originally called the Fuller Building.

Madison Square Park★ – *Madison Ave. - Ⓜ 23 St.* Once at the heart of a very elegant district, this vast square makes a pleasant stop for a picnic.

Museum of Sex★ – *233 5th Ave. - Ⓜ 28 St. - www.museumofsex.com - 10h-21h (21h Fri-Sat) - $17.50 (weekdays before 13h), $19.50 (weekdays after 13h purchased online), $20.50 - under 18s prohibited.* This museum traces the history of the pornography industry in New York from the first pin-ups of the 19C films and pornographic maga...

Stroll through the historic district of Chelsea and the Hudson River docks, where old warehouses have been converted into art galleries, then return to the gigantic skyscrapers and hurly burly of Broadway.

VISIT

Empire State Building

Chelsea Historic District★ –
M *23 St.* Like the English Chelsea, this is a place of quiet streets flanked by tall buildings. The main focus lies between 9th and 10th Avenues, along 20th, 21st and 22nd Streets. The best preserved buildings are on **Cushman Row★** (*406-418 West 20th St.*).

Gallery District★★ – M *23 St.* This is THE neighborhood for art galleries. Start on the south by 20th St. and go up as far as 27th St.

Madison Square Garden –
M *Penn Station - www.thegarden.com.* Sitting atop Penn Station, this huge arena hosts concerts as well as hockey and basketball games.

Empire State Building★★★ –
350, 5th Ave. – M *34 St-Herald Sq. - www. esbnyc.com - 8h-2h - observatory on 102th level: $46.* This legendary skyscraper is one of the highest in the city (*443m with the antenna*). The spectacular view from the top presents a great photo opportunity.

Broadway★ – M *34 St-Herald Sq., Times Sq., 50 St.* New York's most famous street, Broadway is the spine of the Theater District. Since the 19C, nearly 80 theaters have spread along the streets Broadway, in an area ranging from 6th to 8th Avenue between 40th and 57th Streets. Today 40 renovated theaters have successfully re-opened thanks to the success of musicals. At no.432 on 44th Street, is the **Actors Studio** where Dustin Hoffman and Al Pacino studied.

Times Square★★ – *Junction of Broadway and 7th Ave.* – M *Times Sq.* Sometimes referred to as the "Crossroads of the World", Times Square is the heart of the Theater District and one of the world's busiest pedestrian intersections.

Morgan Library★★ – *225 Madison Ave.* - M *Grand Central, 42 St. - www. themorgan.org - 10h30-17h (Fri 21h, free from 19h), Sat 10h-18h, Sun 11h-18h - closed Mon - $20.* The wealth of literary manuscripts and sheet music here is amazing including originals by Mozart, Galileo and Edgar Allan Poe.

New York Public Library★ –
5th Ave. – M *5th Ave. - 10h-18h (Tue-Wed 20h), Sun 13h-17h.* One of the largest libraries in the world, the flagship building in the New York Public Library system is also a historic landmark in Midtown Manhattan.

Grand Central Terminal★★ –
M *Grand Central.* Behind the imposing Beaux Arts façade this station concourse is topped with a painted and electrified ceiling depicting the constellations.

Chrysler Building★★★ – *Corner of 42nd St. and Lexington Ave.* – M *Grand Central, 42 St.* With its slender spire and elegant Art Deco style, this is undoubtedly the most beautiful skyscraper in New York, erected in 1930 for the automobile industrialist Walter Chrysler.

United Nations Headquarters★★ – *Between 42nd and 48th St. - Ⓜ Grand Central - guided visits only: Mon-Fri 9h15-16h15 - buy tickets online at http://visit.un.org/fr - $18.* Visit the UN headquarters for a glimpse of global diplomacy at work.

WHERE TO EAT

Ⓐ **WHERE TO PICNIC?** Backed by the Public Library, **Bryant Park** (Ⓜ *5th Ave.*) is ideal for a picnic break.

⑩ Kung Fu Little Steamed Buns Ramen – *811 8th Ave. - Ⓜ 50 St. - ℘ 917 388 2555 - www.kungfulittlesteamed bunsramen.com - noodles from $10.* Noodle dishes, soups and excellent dumplings are the highlights here.

⑥⑨ Mandoo Bar – *2 West 32nd St. - Ⓜ 34 St. - ℘ 212 279 3075 - http://mandoo barnyc.com - dishes $5-12.* Dumplings, fried or steamed, are the specialty of this tiny Korean restaurant.

④⑧ Oyster Bar – *Grand Central Terminal - Ⓜ Grand Central - ℘ 212 490 6650 - www.oysterbarny.com - dishes $20-35.* The best place in town to try seafood.

⑤⑧ Shake Shack – *691 8th Ave. - Ⓜ 42 St. - ℘ 646 435 0135 - www.shake shack.com - burgers from $4.* Satisfy your burger cravings at this outlet of the gourmet–fast food chain.

⑦⓪ Virgil's – *152 West 44th St. - Ⓜ Time Square - ℘ 212 921 9494 - www.virgilsbbq.com - dishes $14-30.* Texas classics like beef brisket are the specialty here.

TAKE A BREAK

④ Bryant Park Hotel – *40 West 40th St. - Ⓜ 5th Ave.* This fascinating building houses a luxury hotel whose bar is famous for cocktails and DJs.

⑦ The Campbell Apartment – *Grand Central Terminal, 15 Vanderbilt Ave.- Ⓜ Grand Central.* The opulent office of

Broadway

an early-20C businessman is transformed into a stylish cocktail bar.

SHOPPING

㊾ Brooks Brothers – *346 Madison Ave. - Ⓜ 5th Ave.* This is the home of the classic suit, worn by film stars of the 1950s to today's businessmen. You'll also find custom and readymade suits, shirts and ties.

㊿ B&H – *429 9th Ave - Ⓜ 34th St./ Penn Station.* A photography mecca, this is *the* place to find quality used equipment at reasonable prices.

⑦⑤ Macy's – *151 West 34th St. - Ⓜ 34 St., Penn Station.* This sprawling 10-floor department store will satisfy all *fashion addicts*.

⑧⑨ OMG – *270 West 38th St. - Ⓜ 34 St., Penn Station.* Brand-name jeans and T-shirts at bargain prices.

NIGHTLIFE

⑦④ B. B. King Blues Club – *237 West 42nd St. - Ⓜ 42 St. - www.bbking blues.com.* Enjoy quality concerts in one of NYC's premier Live Music Venues and Supperclubs.

⑨⓪ Marquee – *289 10th Ave. - Ⓜ 23 St.* Chic club, frequented by celebrities.

Addresses described in neighboring sections:
⑩⑥ ⑩⑧ ⑨⑦ ⑩④ ⑩ ⑱ ▶ 5
⑬⑧ ⑬④ ⑰ ㊿ ⑦⑥ ⑧④ ▶ 7

© stu99/iStockphoto.com

12th Ave
12th Ave
11th Ave
10th Ave
9th Ave
8th Ave
Broadway
7th Ave
57 St
7 Av

W 56th St

W 54th St
DE WITT CLINTON PARK
West
W 53rd St
MIDTOWN WEST
W 53rd St
52nd

N River Piers
50th
W 51st St
W 51st St
50 St
50 St
W 51st St

Pier 90
11th Ave
W 49th St
Street
W 50th St
49 St

Pier 88
12th Ave
W 48th St
HELL'S KITCHEN
30
GENERAL ELEC BUILDING

Intrepid Sea-Air-Space Museum
Pier 86
W 47th St
W 47th St

W 46th St
W 46th St
THEATER DISTRICT

W 45th St
W 45th St
W 45th St

44th
Ave
Times Square
58
70

Pier 83
W 43rd St
Street
42 St-Port Authority Bus Terminal
74
Times Square-42 S

CIRCLE LINE FERRY TERMINAL
42nd
Street
Madame Tussauds Wax Museum

W 40th St
10th Ave
9th Ave
Port Authority Bus Terminal
Times Square-42

W 39th St
W 39th St
8th Ave

HUDSON RIVER
W 38th St
Hell's Kitchen Flea Market
89
7th

Jacob K. Javits Convention Center
11th Ave
W 36th St
W 37th St
GARMENT DISTRICT

W 35th St
W 35th St
W 35th St
Penn Station
Macy

W 34th St
58
8th
Penn Statio

High Line
10th Ave
9th Ave
33rd
Penn Station

Madison Square Garden
Penn Station
W 32
W 31st St

W 30th St
Dyer Ave
W 30th St
W 3

W 29th St
W 29th St
W 29th St
W 30

Starrett-Lehigh Building
W 28th St
CHELSEA PARK
8th
W 28th St
28 S

W 27th St
10th Ave
90
W 27th St

GALLERY DISTRICT
9th Ave
W 26th St
Fashion Institute of Technology Museum

W 25th St

W 24th St
W 24th St
W 24th St
W 2
23 St

W 23rd St
23rd
23 St

Chelsea Historic District
Chelsea Hotel

W 21st St
Cushman Row
CHELSEA
Ave

Chelsea
W 19th St
W 19th St
Rubin Museum of Ar

W 18th St
18th St
W 18th St
W 17th St
W 17th St

Piers
Ave
4

0   200   400 m

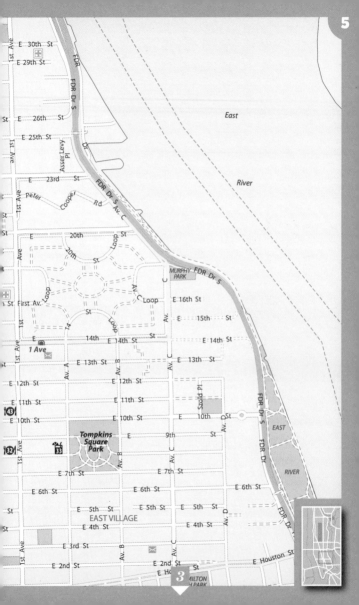

1st Ave
E 30th St
E 29th St
FDR Dr S
FDR
E 26th St
St
E 25th St
1st Ave
Asser Levy Pl
Dr
E 23rd St
FDR Dr S Av. C
Peter
Cooper
Rd
St
1st Ave
E 20th St
Loop
St
20th
St
St
Ave
Loop
Av. C Loop
St First Av.
Loop
1st
14th
St
Av. C
Loop
St
MURPHY PARK
FDR Dr S
E 16th St
E 15th St
Av.
E 14th St
E 14th St
1 Ave
14th St
E 14th St
E 13th St
Av. B
Av. C
E 13th St
E 12th St
E 12th St
E 11th St
E 11th St
[43]
E 10th St
E 10th St
Szold Pl
E 10th St
Av. D
EAST
FDR Dr S
[32]
1st Ave
E 9th St
Av. C
St
Tompkins Square Park
[33]
E 7th St
Av. B
E 7th St
Av. C
E 6th St
E 6th St
E 6th St
FDR Dr
RIVER
St
E 5th St
E 5th St
E 5th St
EAST VILLAGE
E 4th St
E 4th St
Av. D
St
E 3rd St
Av. B
E 2nd St
Av. C
E 2nd St
E Houston St
E Ho
3
AILTON H PARK

East

River

EAST

RIVER

North of midtown, Rockefeller Center is another New York icon. Bordering Central Park, the Upper West Side has attracted the high society of the artistic and literary world with the sound of jazz, opera and exotic rhythms.

VISIT

Rockefeller Center★★★ – *5th Ave. -* Ⓜ *5th Ave. - www.rockefellercenter.com.* A city within the city! The first example of great architectural and urban design in New York includes twenty buildings around a central plaza, with a sunken garden, iconic sculptures and an ice rink in winter.

Top of the Rock★★★ – *Enter from 50th St. -* Ⓜ *5th Ave. - 8h-0h, elevator 8h-0h - www.topoftherocknyc.com - $34.* Rising over three glazed floors, the splendid atrium presents a history of Rockefeller Center. The observatory offers a panoramic view of Midtown.

Saint Patrick's Cathedral★★ – *5th Ave. -* Ⓜ *5th Ave.* One of the first major neo-Gothic churches in the United States (1879) is now wedged between towering highrises.

Radio City Music Hall★ – *1260, 6th Ave. -* Ⓜ *47-50 Sts. - www.radiocity.com.* Characteristic of Art Deco style, this massive indoor theater hosts concerts and a famous holiday show.

Museum of Modern Art (MoMA)★★★ – *11 West 53rd St. -* Ⓜ *5 Ave., 57 St. - www.moma.org - 10h30 -17h30 (Fri 20h, free from 16h) - closed Tue - $25.* One of the world's most famous museums, MoMA's incredible concentration of masterpieces ensures a fascinating stroll through art from the mid-19C to today.

Carnegie Hall – *156 West 57th St. -* Ⓜ *57 St. - www.carnegiehall.org.* Built in a neo-Renaissance style, this famous concert hall was inaugurated in 1891 under the baton of Tchaikovsky.

Museum of Modern Art

Columbus Circle – Ⓜ *59 St.* At the southwest corner of Central Park, this intersection marks the beginning of the Upper West Side. It is bordered by the imposing **Time Warner Center** and the **Museum of Arts and Design★**, which houses a superb collection of decorative arts (*www.madmuseum.org - daily except Mon 10h-18h, Thu-Fri 21h - $16, pay as you wish Thu from 18h*).

Lincoln Center★ – *Broadway -* Ⓜ *66 St. - www.lincolncenter.org.* This huge cultural complex houses the Metropolitan Opera, Avery Fisher Hall, the New York State Theater, the Juilliard School and more.

American Folk Art Museum★★ – *2 Lincoln Sq., Columbus Ave. -* Ⓜ *66 St. - folkartmuseum.org - 11h30-19h, Fri 12h -19h30, Sun 12h-18h - closed Mon - free.* Often overlooked, this museum's rich collection features a wealth of American folk art, from colonial needlepoint to 20C Outsider Art.

New-York Historical Society★★ – *170 Central Park West -* Ⓜ *81 St. - 10h-18h (Fri 8h, pay-as-you-wish from 18h) - closed Mon - $21.* Founded in 1804 to preserve the history of the city, the Society boasts an excellent collection of fine art and paintings of the Hudson School.

American Museum of Natural History★★★ – *Central Park West -* Ⓜ *81 St. - www.amnh.org - 10h-17h45 - $32 (suggested admission).* This huge, spectacular museum houses over

30 million fossils, both animal and mineral, plus a staggering array of other earth science displays.

WHERE TO EAT

☺ **WHERE TO PICNIC? Central Park** (Ⓜ *59 St., 86 St., 5th Ave.*) is self-evident. **Riverside Park** (Ⓜ *79 St.*) on the banks of the Hudson, is also a good option: pick up food for a picnic at **Zabar's** 88 (*2245 Broadway*, Ⓜ *79 St.*).

🍴13 **Dean & Deluca** – *1 Rockefeller Plaza* - Ⓜ *47-50 Sts.* - ☎ *212 664 1372 - www.deandeluca.com - 7h-19h.* A gourmet cafeteria for sandwiches, quiches, salads (*$10/12*), etc.

🍴120 **Five Napkin Burger** – *2315 Broadway* - Ⓜ *86 St.* - ☎ *212 333 4488 - http://5napkinburger.com - dishes $10-18.* Tasty burgers are the star here and there's a full bar too.

🍴128 **Izakaya ida** – *141 West 72nd St.* - Ⓜ *72nd St.* - ☎ *212 580 1600 -www. izakayaida.com - dishes $6-22.* Japanese gastropub with delicious, well-priced lunch sets.

🍴153 **Le Pain Quotidien** – *922 7th Ave.* - Ⓜ *59 St. - Columbus Circle* - ☎ *212 757 0775 - around $15.* Look for quality baked goods and light fare at this chain outlet.

🍴153 **PJ Clarke's** – *915 3rd Ave.* - Ⓜ *Lexington Ave.-53 St.* - ☎ *212 317 1616 - www.pjclarkes.com - dishes $15-40.* Once frequented by Frank Sinatra and Jackie Onassis, this historic pub is known for its burgers.

TAKE A BREAK

🍴17 **King Cole Bar** – *St. Regis Hotel - 2 East 55th St.* - Ⓜ *5th Ave.* Best known for its namesake mural, this warm wood hotel bar sports a timeless sophistication.

Central Park from Top of the Rock

SHOPPING

🛍50 **American Girl Place** – *609, 5th Ave.* - Ⓜ *47-50 Sts, 5th Ave.* AG fans do not want to miss this flagship store complete with cafe and "beauty salon."

🛍53 **Bergdorf Goodman** – *754, 5th Ave.* - Ⓜ *5th Ave.* Located on both sides of the 5th Avenue, this is one of New York's premier temples of chic luxury, full of understated elegance to the last accessory.

🛍76 **Magpie** – *488 Amsterdam Ave.* - Ⓜ *86 St.* Neighborhood boutique selling home goods, accessories, and gifts fair trade, local, organic, and handmade.

🛍84 **Saks 5th Ave** – *611 5th Ave.* - Ⓜ *5th Ave.* A store that brings together the latest designer women's and men's apparel, shoes, handbags, beauty products and much more, spread across on ten floors.

NIGHTLIFE

🎵75 **Beacon Theatre** – *2124 Broadway* - Ⓜ *72 St. - www.beacontheatre.com.* An institution since 1929! Many top artists have appeared in this Art Deco room from Bob Dylan to Tina Turner.

Addresses described in section 8:
7 10 119 134 139 163 5 50 51
51 54 63 72 81 98

© Jon Arnold/hemis.fr

Jacqueline
Kennedy
Onassis
Reservoir

W 93rd St
W 92nd St
W 91st St
W 90th St

W 89th St
W 88th St
W 87th St
W 86th St
W 85th St

Riverside Park

West Dr

W 86th

Transverse

86 St

86 St

CLEOPATRAS
NEEDLE

W 85th St

West Dr

W 84th St
W 83rd St
W 82nd St

20
76

81 St-Museum
of Natural History

Shakespeare
Garden

Turtle Pond

W 81st St
AMERICAN
MUSEUM
OF NATURAL
HISTORY

Belvedere
Castle

80th
W 79th St

88

Swedish
Cottage

W 79th St

CENTRAL
PARK

79
St

The Boathouse

The Apthorp

New-York
Historical
Society

The
Lake

Loeb

63

Bow Bridge

75

Verdi
Square

The
Dakota

Bethesda
Fountain
Terrace

Ansonia
Hotel

28

72nd

St

72 St

Majestic
Apartments

RUMSEY
PLAYFIELL

81

W 71st St
W 70th St

SHEEP
MEADOW

SHAKESPEARE
STATUE

W 67th St

American Folk
Art Museum

TAVERN ON
THE GREEN

W 66th St

66 St-Lincoln
Center

CAROUSEL

Center
Dr

THE
DAIRY

W 64th St

W 63rd St

Lincoln
Center

W 64th St

W 63rd St

WOLLMAN
MEMORIAL
RINK

W 61st
Dr

W 62nd

59 St-
Columbus
Circle

UPPER WEST SIDE

THE PLAZ

W 59th St

Columbus Circle

Central

Park

W 58th St

Time
Warner
Center

Museum of
Arts & Design

63

W 57th St

W 57th St

57 St-
7 Av

Carnegie
Hall

57 S

W 56th St
W 55th St
W 54th St
W 53rd St

W 55th St
W 54th St
W 53rd St

7Av

MOMA

West

52nd

N River Piers

DE WITT
CLINTON
PARK

Radio City
Music Hall

W 50th St

Street

50 St

50 St

GENERAL ELEC
BUILDING

Pier 90

0   250   500 m

W 48th St

HELL'S
KITCHEN

6

49 St

W 48th St

HUDSON RIVER

MUSEUM MILE

Jewish Museum

Cooper-Hewitt
Design Museum

E 92nd St
E 91st St
E 90th St

Guggenheim
Museum

Gracie
Mansion

E 88th St
E 87th St
E 86th St

Neue
Galerie

5

34

86 St

86 St

31

E 85th St
E 84th St

CARL
SCHURZ
PARK

METROPOLITAN
MUSEUM
OF ART

E 83rd St
E 82nd St
E 81st St
E 80th St

YORKVILLE

ROOSEVELT

E 79th St
E 78th St

Ukrainian
Institute

ALICE IN
WONDERLAND
STATUE

77 St

8

UPPER EAST SIDE

E 77th St

JOHN JAY
PARK

98

Met Breuer

MODEL
BOATHOUSE

E 74th St
E 73rd St

19

Conservatory
Water

E 73rd St
72 St

E 72nd St

THE FRICK
COLLECTION

E 71st St
E 70th St

Asia Society

ALTO
STATUE

68 St-Hunter
College

E 69th St
E 68th St

CHILDREN'S ZOO

LENOX HILL

Temple Emanu-El

Zoo

72

Lexington Ave-
63 St

7

UPPER EAST SIDE

51

E 63rd St
E 62nd St
E 61st St

Grand Army Plaza

54

63 30

Roosevelt Island Tramway

5 Ave

59 St

Lexington Ave

Ed Koch

Queensboro Brg

53

E 58th St
E 57th St

Bridgemarket

ROOSEVELT
Island

WEST CHANNEL

EAST CHANNEL

Roosevelt Island
Brg

ISLAND

59th St

MIDTOWN
EAST

St Regis
Sheraton

17

53

E 55th St
E 54th St
E 53rd St

5 Ave

E 53rd St

Lexington Ave

St Thomas

St Patrick's
Cathedral

51 St

E 52nd St
E 51st St
E 50th St
E 49th St

84

13

50

ROCKEFELLER CENTER/
TOP OF THE ROCK

TURTLE BAY

The Loeb Boathouse Central Park

54 Le Pain Quotidien – *1131 Madison Ave. -* M *86 St. -* 📞 *212 327 4900 - around $15.* You'll find salads and light fare at affordable prices, plus baked goods at this chain outlet. It's ideal for preparing a picnic.

58 Maya – *191, 1ˢᵗ Ave. -* M *Lexington Ave. -* 📞 *212 585 1818 - www.modern mexicano.com - lunch menu $19, dishes $20-30.* The Mexican cuisine blends the new and the traditional, and comes in a refined setting.

69 The Loeb Boathouse Central Park – *Enter from East 72ⁿᵈ St. -* M *77 St. -* 📞 *212 517 2233 - www.thecentral parkboathouse.com - dishes $25-45.* Beside the lake, the lovely veranda here offers romantic sunsets.

TAKE A BREAK

5 Café Sabarsky at the Neue Gallerie – *1048, 5ᵗʰ Ave. -* M *86 St. - closed Tue.* Adjacent to the museum, this elegant Viennese café serves delicious pastries.

31 Ryan's Daughter – *380 East 85ᵗʰ St. -* M *86 St.* A classic Irish pub atmosphere with darts, billiards, and cheap beer.

30 Serendipity 3 – *225 East 60ᵗʰ St. -* M *59 St.* Once frequented by Andy Warhol, this tea lounge, restaurant and café sports funky kitsch decor.

SHOPPING

Madison Avenue (M *5ᵗʰ Ave., 68 St.*) harbours New York's most exclusive stores, especially towards the north. Prices dip the farther away from the avenue you go, including on **Lexington** and **3rd Avenues** where the options are less spectacular but less exclusive.

51 Barneys – *660 Madison Ave. -* M *5ᵗʰ Ave.* Arguably New York's trendiest department store, Barney's features a nice selection of work by young designers.

54 Bloomingdale's – *At the corner of Lexington Ave. and 59ᵗʰ St. -* M *59 St.* One of New York's most popular stores, it sells almost everything.

63 Dylan's Candy Bar – *1011, 3ʳᵈ Ave. -* M *59 St.* The milkshakes bar, candy, lollipops and chocolates are hard to resist, whatever your age!

72 Jimmy Choo – *716 Madison Ave. -* M *5ᵗʰ Ave.* A very fashionable address for footwear fiends.

NIGHTLIFE

In **Central Park**, from June to August, the **Shakespeare in the Park Festival** presents free classical theater performances (*www.shakespeareinthepark.org*). From May to September, **Central Park Summer Stage** presents free concerts at **Rumsey Playfield 81** (*www.summerstage.org).*

98 Iggy's – *1452, 2ⁿᵈ Ave. -* M *77 St.* A boisterous club that stands in contrast to the staid side of the neighborhood, with Karaoke evenings featuring the latest hits.

Addresses described in neighboring sections:

31 53 66 ▶ 7

2 ▶ 9

not admitted. This Beaux Arts-style building houses the German and Austrian art collections of Robert Lauder and Serge Sabarsky including works by Schiele, Klimt, Kokoschka, Kandinsky.

Guggenheim Museum★★ –

1071, 5th Ave. - Ⓜ 86 St. - 10h-17h45 (Sat 19h45) - closed Thu - $25; pay-as-you-wish Sat from 17h45) This architectural masterpiece was designed by Frank Lloyd Wright in 1943 to house the modern art collection of Solomon R. Guggenheim. Inside, the 400m-long spiral ramp provides access to some 6,000 works and the **Kandinsky Gallery★★★**, which includes 200 works of the artist.

Cooper-Hewitt Design Museum★★

– *2 East 91st St. - Ⓜ 86 St. - 10h-18h (Sat 21h) - $18 (pay-as-you-wish Sat from 18h).* Set in an imposing 64-room mansion this museum is dedicated to decorative arts, highlighting design across cultures, eras and continents.

Jewish Museum★ –

1109, 5th Ave. Ⓜ 96 St. - 11h-17h45 (Thu 20h) - closed Wed - $15 (pay-as-you-wish Thu 17h-20h; free Saturdays). This museum recounts 4,000 years of Jewish history through some 28,000 objects including magnificent bindings, textiles and ancient ritual vessels.

El Museo del Barrio★ –

1230, 5th Ave. - Ⓜ 103 St. - Wed-Sat 11h-18h - contribution suggested $9. Founded in 1969 on the edge of Hispanic Harlem, this museum is dedicated to Latin American and Caribbean cultures.

Roosevelt Island Tramway★ –

2nd Ave. - Ⓜ Lexington Ave. - Sun-Thu 6h-2h, Fri-Sat 6h-3h30 - use a MetroCard. Parallel to Queensboro Bridge, this cablecar offers a beautiful view of Manhattan.

Gracie Mansion★ –

East End Ave. (opposite 89th St.) - Ⓜ 86 St. - www.nyc.gov - guided visits Wed at 10h, 11h, 13h and 14h - reservation essential. ☎ 212 570 4773 - $7. The official residence of the Mayor of New York is a charming Federal-style manor house (1799) with covered galleries and green shutters.

WHERE TO EAT

🍴 **WHERE TO PICNIC? Central Park** (Ⓜ 5th Ave., Columbus Circle) is a must. Families will head to the spacious lawns of **Sheep Meadow**; with little ones, head for the **zoo** to find the nearby playgrounds. Romantics will choose the lake or reservoir.

7️ Burger Heaven – *804 Lexington Ave. - Ⓜ Lexington Ave.-63 St. - ☎ 212 838 3580 - www.burgerheaven.com - dishes $9-16.* An unassuming address, but with plenty of choice of inexpensive salads and hearty burgers.

8️ Café Carlyle – *35 East 76th St. – Ⓜ 77 St. - ☎ 212 744 1600 - www.rosewoodhotels.com - dishes $34-50.* New York celebrity society comes out to be seen at this chic nightspot, known for its top-quality jazz performances. Woody Allen visits from time to time.

19️ EJ's Luncheonette – *1271, 3rd Ave. - Ⓜ 77 St. - ☎ 212 472 0600 - www.ejsluncheonette.com - dishes $10-15, brunch from $14.* Famous for its brunch, this family restaurant serves delicious pancakes, eggs and omelettes.

Roosevelt Island Tramway

A huge expanse of green surrounded by skyscrapers, Central Park is an oasis for a long walk or a picnic. To the east, on the stretch of 5th Avenue adjacent to the park, stately mansions house prestigious museums.

VISIT

Central Park★★★ – M *5th Ave, Columbus Circle, Cathedral Pkwy, Central Park N.* With 841 acres, Central Park is the green lung of New York, where people take a break from the city without actually leaving it.

Central Park Zoo – *Central Park -* M *5th Ave. - 10h-17h (Nov-Mar 16h30) - $18.* More than 450 animals in this zoo are divided into three major climatic zones (temperate, tropical, polar).

Bethesda Fountain Terrace★ – *Central Park -* M *72 St.* Reached along the Mall, a majestic driveway shaded by giant elms, this plaza with its central fountain looks like a Spanish courtyard.

The Lake★★ – *Central Park -* M *72 St.* Skirting the lake on the right, you reach the **Loeb Boathouse**, where you can rent row boats or sit for a meal (** Where to Eat**). The graceful **Bow Bridge★★** accesses the northern end of the lake.

Jacqueline Kennedy Onassis Reservoir★ – *Central Park -* M *86 St., 96 St.* This is one of the most popular places for joggers.

5th Avenue★ – M *5th Ave.* An enduring symbol of ritzy New York, this avenue was once home to the city's largest mansions and has evolved into one of department stores and luxury boutiques. The stretch that extends along Central Park is **Museum Mile★★★**, where you'll find one of world's best concentrations of museums.

Metropolitan Museum of Art

Temple Emanu-El★ – M *5th Ave. - Sun-Thu 10h30-16h30.* This Romanesque-Mauresco-Byzantine style synagogue (1929) is one of the largest in the world.

The Frick Collection★★★ – *1 East 70th St. -* M *68 St.-Hunter College - www.frick.org - 10h-18h, Sun 11h-17h - closed Mon - $22 (free Wed 14h-18h and first Fri of the month 18h-21h, except Sept and Jan)- under 10s not admitted.* A great place to learn about classical painting, the Frick features works by Boucher, Gainsborough and Hogarth.

Asia Society and Museum★★ – *725 Park Ave. -* M *68 St.-Hunter College - www.asiasociety.org - 11h-18h - closed Mon - $12 (free Fri 18-21h Sept-June).* Set in a remarkable building, this museum's superbly highlighted collections cover the entire Asian continent.

Met Breuer★★ – *945 Madison Ave. -* M *77 St. - 10h-17h30 (Fri-Sat 21h) - $25 suggested admission (incl. Cloisters, Met Breuer, Met).* In the Whitney's former building is the Met's modern and contemporary art outpost.

Metropolitan Museum of Arts (Met)★★★ – M *5th Ave. -* M *86 St. - 10h-17h30 (Fri-Sat 21h) - $25 suggested admission.* This renowned museum's massive collections—two million objects divided into 19 sections—that extend from Sumerian antiquities to the art of the 20C.

Neue Galerie★ – *1048 5th Ave. - 86 St. - 11h-18h - closed Tue-Wed - $20 (free first Friday of the month 18h-20h - under 12s*

WHERE TO EAT

⊕ WHERE TO PICNIC? The charming **Marcus Garvey Park** (Ⓜ *125th St.*) is a convenient option. You can also join **Riverside Park** (Ⓜ *Cathedral Pkwy*) along the Hudson, or head to **Central Park** or around the Harlem Meer.

② **Amor Cubano** – *2018, 3rd Ave. -* Ⓜ *110 St. -* ☎ *212 996 1220 - www. amorcubanorestaurant.com - lunch menu $15, dishes $18-26 - reservations advised in the evening.* Expect a 100% Cuban atmosphere, warm and highly charged, with traditional dishes, mojitos and good live music.

③ **Amy Ruth's** – *113 West 116th St. -* Ⓜ *116 St. -* ☎ *212 280 8779 - www.amyruth sharlem.com - dishes $13-23.* Don't be dissuaded by the impersonal setting: this is the best place to try the delicious cuisine of the southern states.

㊶ **Harlem Public** – *3612 Broadway. -* Ⓜ *145 St. -* ☎ *212 939 9404 - www. spoonbreadinc.com - dishes $11-28.* Hopping neighborhood joint with outdoor seating and New American pub grub.

㊿ **Patsy's** – *2287, 1st Ave. -* Ⓜ *116 St. -* ☎ *212 534 9783 - www.thepatsyspizza.com - dishes $10-25.* Some of the city's best coal-fired pizza since 1933. Eat in or take away.

> ### *Attend a Gospel Service*
> *Do not miss the Sunday morning gospel services (usually 9h and 11h), held in Baptist churches such as* **Abyssinian Baptist Church ㊲** *(132 W 138th St. -* Ⓜ *135 St.),* **Canaan Baptist Church ㊿** *(132 W 116th St. -* Ⓜ *116 St.) or* **First Corinthian Baptist Church ㊷** *(1912 Adam Clayton Powell Jr Blvd -* Ⓜ *116 St.).*

㊅ **Uptown Juice Bar** – *14 East 125th St. -* Ⓜ *Harlem-125 St. -* ☎ *212 987 2660 - www.uptownvegjuicebar.com - dishes around $10.* Everything here is vegetarian, nourishing and, for NYC, very cheap.

TAKE A BREAK

⑭ **Hungarian Pastry Shop** – *1030 Amsterdam Ave. -* Ⓜ *Cathedral Pkwy.* A warm Hungarian coffee and pastry shop used by numerous filmmakers including Woody Allen.

SHOPPING

㊹ **The Store at the Studio Museum** – *144 West 125th St. -* Ⓜ *125 St.* Interesting selection of books on African-American art and black culture.

NIGHTLIFE

㊓ **Apollo Theater** – *253 West 125th St. -* Ⓜ *125 St. - www.apollotheater.com.* THE legendary venue for listening to jazz, R&B and soul. The greats play here from time to time, but Amateur Night (*Wed. 7h30*) reveals the talent of tomorrow.

�89 **Smoke Jazz Club** – *2751 Broadway -* Ⓜ *Cathedral Pkwy - www.smokejazz.com - dinner show at 19h, 21h and 22h30, brunch jazz Sun 11h-16h.* One of the most interesting Uptown jazz scenes, mixing classic and innovative artists.

Forget the idealized image of the cradle of jazz and the specter of a violent, blighted cityscape, Harlem today has changed and the bourgeoisie have settled in. The intelligentsia aren't far away either, south of Morningside Heights near Columbia University.

Columbia University

VISIT

Studio Museum in Harlem★ –
144 West 125th St. - Ⓜ 125 St. - Thu-Fri 12h-21h, Sat 10h-18h, Sun 12h-18h - $7 (free Sun). With beautiful exhibitions, ranging from folk art to videos, this museum is dedicated to African-American art and local artists.

Marcus Garvey Park★ – *Between*
West 124th and 119th St. - Ⓜ Harlem-125 St. On the west side of this lovely park, you will see a row of well-renovated brownstones (houses in red brick or brownstone), allowing you to imagine bourgeois Harlem in the late 19C.

Apollo Theater★ – *253 West 125th St. -*
Ⓜ *125 St.* Since 1934 this has been the temple of black music, especially jazz, and one of the most popular venues in New York. Louis Armstrong, Aretha Franklin and James Brown have all performed here.

Schomburg Center for Research in Black Culture★ – *515 Malcolm X*
Blvd - Ⓜ *135 St. - Tue-Wed 12h-20h, Thu-Fri 12h-18h, Sat 10h-18h – free.* The center, part of the city's library system, has more than 5 million documents illustrating the culture, history, heritage and identity of the African American population.

Strivers Row – *West 138th and*
139th St. - Ⓜ *135 St.* In these beautiful brownstones the rising black middle class settled in the 1920s. The Georgian style mansions and neo-Renaissance have been gradually given a face-lift.

Cathedral of Saint John The Divine★★ – *1047 Amsterdam Ave. -*
Ⓜ *Cathedral Pkwy.* Today something of a cultural center, the cathedral hosts art shows and musical performances. Behind the choir, the center of the chapel houses a silver triptych designed by Keith Haring (1989).

Columbia University★★ – *Entrance*
on Broadway, to 116th St. - Ⓜ *116 St.-Columbia University.* Founded in 1754, Columbia is one of the most prestigious private universities in the country. The **Low Memorial Library★** (1895) recalls the Roman Pantheon.

Riverside Park★★ – Ⓜ *Cathedral*
Pkwy. This park stretches along the Hudson River, down Riverside Drive, from 72nd Street up to 155th. The fun part is located south of 100th Street, including the English Garden (*91st St.*).

Riverside Church★★ – *Riverside Dr.*
and 120th St. - Ⓜ *116 St.-Columbia University.* An imposing neo-Gothic structure, the church has two 16C stained-glass windows from the Cathedral of Bruges and a carillon of 74 bells. From its steeple there are beautiful views of the Hudson.

General Grant National Memorial★ – *Riverside Dr. -* Ⓜ *116 St.-*
Columbia University - reception: 9h-17h ; mausoleum: 10h-11h, 12h-13h, 14h-15h and 16h-17h - closed Tue - free. A monument (1896) to Ulysses S. Grant, US president from 1869 to 1877.

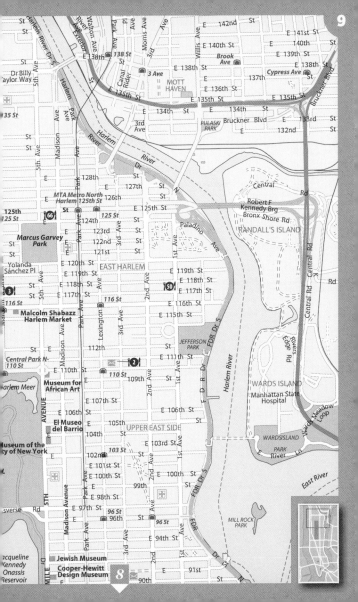

are a true delight and the espresso is tasty, but those with robust appetites will be disappointed.

29 Reunion – *544 Union Ave. -* Ⓜ *Bedford Ave.* Bright café serving colorful, healthy, modern Aussie-Israeli-American fare.

SHOPPING

60 Beacon's Closet – *92 5th Ave. -* Ⓜ *Pacific St.* At this thrift store, you can unearth vintage clothing for just a handful of dollars. There's a second Brooklyn location at 23 Bogart St. *(not on map -* Ⓜ *Morgan Ave.).*

89 Brooklyn Flea Markets – *Sun 10h-18h Apr-Oct - DUMBO (80 Pearl St.),* Ⓜ *High St.-Brooklyn Bridge. This* flea market reflects bohemian and trendy Brooklyn spirit, offering vintage clothing, furniture built with recycled materials, handmade jewelry and the like.

64 Earwax Records – *not on map -* 167 North 9th St., Williamsburg - Ⓜ *Bedford Ave.* Head here to browse a collection of hard-to-find vinyl.

86 Spring – *126 A Front St. -* Ⓜ *York St. - closed Mon-Tue.* This gallery features goods created by Brooklyn designers.

87 Picnic – *192 Amity St. -* Ⓜ *Bergen St. - closed Mon.* Adorable kids clothing, accessories, and NYC-themed toys and books.

Take a boat to Brooklyn
On a warm day, a ferry ride between Manhattan and Brooklyn is a treat ($2.75). You can pick up the ferries at **Pier 11** *in Manhattan and, in Brooklyn, in Williamsburg, Brooklyn Bridge Park, and DUMBO. www.ferry.nyc*

NIGHTLIFE

78 Brooklyn Academy of Music (BAM) – *30 Lafayette Ave. -* Ⓜ *Fulton St. - www.bam.org.* A cultural institution considered the Mecca of avant-garde New York, BAM hosts contemporary ballets, opera, physical theater, visual art, comedy, galas, parties and quality musical creations.

86 Output – *not on map - 74 Wythe Ave., Williamsburg - www.outputclub.com.* Ⓜ *Nassau Ave.* Specialized programming and striking lights set the scene for DJ sessions, and rooftop cocktails with wonderful views of Manhattan *(no entry fee).*

93 The Ides Bar – *not on map - Wythe Hotel - 80 Wythe Ave., Williamsburg - http://wythehotel.com/the-ides.* Ⓜ *Nassau Ave.* This bar is perched on the rooftop of the hip Wythe Hotel (6th floor), a small industrial-vintage brick gem that was once a huge warehouse. Expect a low-key, trendy scene and a great view of Manhattan. Entry is first come, first served... don't be late.

94 The Knitting Factory – *361 Metropolitan Ave. -* Ⓜ *Marcy Ave. - www.knittingfactory.com.* Equal parts music room and bar, this longtime club features eclectic programming and a great atmosphere.

96 Union Pool – *not on map - 484 Union Ave., Williamsburg -* Ⓜ *Lorimer St. - www.union-pool.com.* A Williamsburg must, both a bar and concert hall, plus a large garden with fairy lights where you can eat tacos while you drink.

Bedford Avenue, Williamsburg

bagels of all kinds and various toppings creamy, sweet or savory, plus soups and salads.

6 Cafe Steinhof – *Corner of 7th Ave. and 14th St.* - **M** *7 Ave.* - ☎ *718 369 7776 - cafesteinhof.com - dishes $10-17.* Cozy Austrian atmosphere with a fine selection of beers and robust dishes. Film show on Sunday night.

10 Cubana Café – *272 Smith St.* - **M** *Carroll St.* - ☎ *718 858 3980 - www.cubanacafenyc.com - dishes $10-14.* Cuban restaurant serving hearty dishes, like coconut shrimp, plantains and pork plus sandwiches.

14 Diner – *85 Broadway* - **M** *Marcy Ave.* - ☎ *718 486 3077 - www.dinernyc.com - dishes $15-25.* Set in an old Art deco diner under the Williamsburg Bridge, this restaurant offers more creative American cuisine than its name suggests. No reservations; first come, first served.

21 Fornino – *not on the map - 187 Bedford Ave., Williamsburg* - **M** *Bedford Ave* - ☎ *718 384 6004 - www.fornino.com - pizzas $10-22.* Excellent thin-crust pizzas cooked in a wood fired oven with creative, gourmet toppings.

26 Juliana's – *19 Old Fulton St.* - **M** *High St., York St.* - ☎ *718 596-6700 - julianaspizza.com - pizzas $15-20.* Located under the Brooklyn Bridge, Juliana's is one of Brooklyn's most famous pizzerias.

39 Meatball Shop – *not on map - 170 Bedford Ave., Williamsburg* - **M** *Bedford Ave.* - ☎ *718 551 0520 - www.themeatballshop.com - around $10.* Meatballs in a variety of styles and permutations are the focus here. You choose the meat, the sauce and the way they're served.

40 Miriam – *79, 5th Ave.* - **M** *Pacific St.* - ☎ *718 622 2250 - www.miriamrestaurant.com - dishes $10-20.* The delicious Israeli cuisine here is matched by friendly service.

52 Peter Luger – *178 Broadway* - **M** *Marcy Ave.* - ☎ *718 387 7400 - http:// peterluger.com - lunch: dishes $12-20; evenings: steak around $40 - reservation essential.* Some say this historic institution serves the best steak in New York.

TAKE A BREAK

1 Almondine – *85 Water St.* - **M** *York St.* - ☎ *718 797 5026 - www. almondinebakery.com.* French bakery where you can taste strawberry tarts, éclairs, mille-feuille, fruit tart, pies and great sandwiches.

5 Brooklyn Brewery – *not on map - 79 N, 11th St., Williamsburg* - **M** *Bedford Ave.* A well-known brewery thanks to its flagship beer, Brooklyn Lager. Stop by the bar to sample rarer brews *(Happy Hour Fri 18h-23h).* Tasting tours available *(Mon-Thu 17h-19h, Sat 13h-17h, 13h-16h Sun. about $10).*

9 Chocolate Room – *82 5th Ave.* - **M** *Pacific St.* Here, almost everything is chocolate, including hot and cold drinks and, of course, desserts. There's one exception to the rule: you can order a glass of sweet wine or a beer.

24 One Girl Cookies – *68 Dean St.* - **M** *Bergen St.* Turquoise and impeccable stainless steel make for a simple, feminine setting. The cookies

Brooklyn embodies the marriage of chic style and hip urbanity with a storied past: Brooklyn Heights and its bourgeois homes, Dumbo and its loft buildings, Williamsburg and its artists, Park Slope and its families—they're all part of the modern Brooklyn.

Brooklyn Bridge

VISIT

Brooklyn Bridge★★★ – Ⓜ *High St.* A real technical feat for the 19C, this famous suspension bridge opened in 1883 to connect Manhattan to Brooklyn. Walk across for spectacular views of Manhattan and the harbour.

Brooklyn Heights★★ – Ⓜ *Clark St., Court St.* This part of Brooklyn was the first area to develop when the connections to Manhattan became easier. From the promenade that overlooks the river, there is a fine panorama of Lower Manhattan and its skyscrapers.

Manhattan Bridge – Ⓜ *York St.* This beautiful blue-painted metal bridge provides the link between Lower Manhattan and Brooklyn's Dumbo neighborhood. The lower level has three lanes, four subway tracks, a pedway and a bike lane.

Dumbo★ – Ⓜ *York St.* Between Brooklyn and Manhattan Bridge, Dumbo (*Down Under the Manhattan Bridge Overpass*) is a former district of factories and warehouses now an upscale address for young BoHos.

Brooklyn Bridge Park/Empire Fulton Ferry Park★★ – Ⓜ *York St.* From this park on the river, you get an unforgettable view of the towers of Manhattan.

Williamsburg★ – Ⓜ *Marcy Ave.* Between street art, concept stores and flea markets, Williamsburg is the trendy showcase of Brooklyn. Stroll along Bedford Avenue and Berry Street, north of Williamsburg Bridge. On Sunday a flea market animates the neighborhood. (⬥ *Shopping*).

Prospect Park★ – Ⓜ *Prospect Park.* This massive green space, designed by the landscape architects of Central Park, includes a small zoo, the **Brooklyn Botanic Garden★** (*Lefferts Historic House - www.bbg*） and an 18C Dutch farm.

Brooklyn Museum of Art★★ – *200 Eastern Parkway -* Ⓜ *Brooklyn Museum - Wed-Sun 11h-18h (Thu 22h) - $16 (suggested admission; free first Sat of the month).* One of the richest art collections in the city is found at this museum, known for its holdings of American paintings and sculpture and Egyptian antiquities.

WHERE TO EAT

🍴 **WHERE TO PICNIC?** Buy salads and sandwiches at **Foragers** ⑱ (*56 Adams St. -* Ⓜ *York St.*) and sit on the grass in **Brooklyn Bridge Park**. If you go to **Brooklyn Museum**, go to **Prospect Park**. In Williamsburg, you can also buy food at **Smorgasburg** (*off map - East River State Park -* Ⓜ *Bedford Ave. - Sat from Apr-Nov*) or Whole Foods (*off map - 238 Bedford Ave,*) and enjoy your lunch overlooking the Manhattan skyline.

🍴 **Bagel World** – *339, 5th Ave. -* Ⓜ *9 St. -* 𝄢 *718 499 1143 - www.bagel worldparkslope.com - less than $10.* Serves

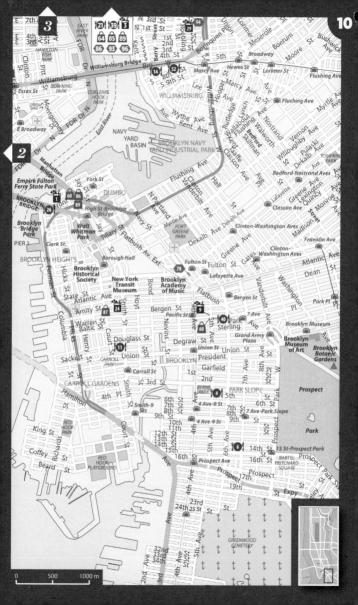

Rates increase at night (20h-5h) and at peak hours (Mon-Fri 16h-20h). To estimate the price of a trip: www.nyccabfare.com.

MONEY & BUDGET

Banks and ATMs - You will find ATMs everywhere, including in smaller shops and delis. Banks are generally open Monday to Friday, 9h to 17h30, sometimes on Saturdays from 9h to noon. Credit cards are widely accepted but are sometimes not accepted in smaller restaurants.

Budget - New York is a particularly expensive destination, especially in terms of accommodation. Allow $250-350 for a night in a comfortable hotel, $15-40 for a seated meal in a good restaurant, $100-300 for a Broadway musical or concert, $7 for a beer, and $8-20 to enter a museum. That said, there are ways to bring costs down significantly, including flat hire through Airbnb or VRBO, Broadway lotteries and last-minute ticket kiosks, and doing research to find lauded but moderately-priced restaurants.

Tipping - Unless the service is included, give between 15 and 20%.

In an emergency

Fire, police, ambulance 24/7: ☏ 911.
Credit card loss: Amex: ☏ 1 800 528 4800. Visa: ☏ 1 800 847 2911. Master Card: ☏ 1 636 722 7111.

British Consulate General - 845 Third Avenue, New York NY 10022. ☏ 1 212 745 0200.

Doctors 24/7: ☏ 1 800 468 3537.

SOS dentist: ☏ 212 998 9458 (week) or 9828 (weekend).

☏ Health care is prohibitively expensive in the US: contact your insurance (CB, support ...) before you go to the hospital (in order to open a case number).

Taxi by the Metropolitan Museum of Art

TIPS

Stock up on **promotional brochures** at the tourist office and at the hotel: many contain discount coupons for attractions. Sites like www.clubfreetime.com, www.timeout.com/ny and www.theskint.com list free activities and events. They also reference a large number of free cultural and sporting activities.

Staten Island Ferry - This free shuttle (⚓ *Section 1*) offers a 20min cruise between Battery Park and Staten Island, with views of the Statue of Liberty and Manhattan.

Cash withdrawals - In McDonald's, ATMs charge a small fee ($0.99 against $3-4 elsewhere).

Food - There are economic ways of eating in New York: pretzels stands or hot dog stalls in the street; fast food outlets (burgers, soups, wraps ...); world cuisine and fresh products in markets (Chelsea Market in particular); supermarkets and delicatessens, etc., where you can eat for $5-10. We indicate the best places to picnic in each district, at the beginning of the "Where to Eat" section.

Free pizza every night until 3h30 in the Alligator Lounge in Brooklyn (600 Metropolitan Ave.) or at the Crocodile Lounge in the East Village (325 East 14th St.).

In restaurants, Early Bird or Pre-theater menus, served early in the evening (17h-19h30), are often less than $30.

GETTING AROUND NEW YORK

Metropolitan Transportation Authority – www.mta.info.

Google Maps (maps.google.com) allows you to visualize and calculate an estimated cost and time of transportation.

Tickets and charges

Buy – In subway stations, MetroCard vending machines or at the counter. In the bus from the driver.

Charges – Valid on buses and subway, a **single ticket** costs $2.75 and is valid only for one trip, including transfers.

The **Pay-Per-Ride Metrocard** is a rechargeable card that you top up as necessary and which functions as a reserve ticket. The **Unlimited Ride Metrocard** available for 7 Days ($31) and 30 Days ($116.50) offers unlimited access to the subway and bus. The **EasyPay MetroCard** works the same way, but will be recharged as and when it is used.

Metro (Subway)

Network – The lines have a number or a letter. To know which platform to take, it's either the direction that counts (*Downtown, Uptown*) or destination (*Brooklyn, Queens*). Once you're through the turnstiles, some stations allow you reverse direction without swiping your card again, but some do not. If you're using an unlimited ride card and you make a mistake, you have to wait 18 minutes

before you can use the card again. Subway lines are local or express. Several lines can use the same platform: check the number or letter displayed in front of the train and on the side.

Times – Subways run 24/7, though some stations are closed at night and some lines don't run on weekends.

Bus

Network – The lines are distinguished by a number. The letter that precedes it indicates the *borough* (neighborhood): M for Manhattan, B for Brooklyn, etc. In Manhattan, the transverse lines bear the number of the street they run along. To request the next stop, press the Stop buttons or the yellow vertical stripes between the windows.

Times – Many lines operate 24/7, but at a very reduced overnight rate.

Cycling

Bike - Cycling on New York streets isn't for the faint of heart, but in parks and protected bike paths it's truly lovely. Information and map: www.nyc.gov/html/dot/html/bicyclists/bicyclists.shtml

Citi Bike - www.citibikenyc.com. City-wide bike-share system ($12/24h, $24/72h for unlimited 30-min rides; no helmet). Most bike shops have hire bikes (average $35/24h)

The **TD Five Boro Bike Tour** takes place in early May, a ride involving some 32,000 cyclists, car-free around all five boroughs of the city (www.bikenewyork.org). The NYC Century Ride, held in September, (biketours.transalt.org/nyccentury) is a 100mi (161km) ride through the city. There are also shorter routes.

Taxi

They are available if the number on their roof light is on. They have a counter and the fare is based on distance traveled + extras ($2.50).

Wall Street station

WHEN TO GO

Seasons

New York has a temperate climate that can be rather wet, characterized by a wide range of temperatures.

Spring and autumn are very pleasant times. In summer, average temperatures are around 86°F during the day.

In winter, temperatures can be below freezing but are just as often in the low 40s°F. Snow storms, high winds and severe temperatures are only occasional.

Calendar of Key Events

Chinese New Year's Festival – *End Jan-early Feb.* Chinese New Year in Chinatown.

Central Brooklyn Jazz Festival – *Apr.* Jazz concerts.

Lesbian and Gay Pride Week – *End Jun.* On 5th Avenue.

Independance Day – *Jul 4.* National Day: fireworks; boat parade at the South Street Seaport.

Greenwich Village Halloween Parade – *Oct 31.* Halloween.

New York Marathon – *Early Nov.*

Macy's Thanksgiving Day Parade – *4th Thu of Nov.* Parade along Broadway, from Central Park West to Herald Square.

Check-list for International Visitors

Formalities: Foreign nationals must possess a printed and or biometric passport (issued before October 26, 2005).

Currency: The US Dollar ($)

Time difference: All year, five hours behind the UK.

Electricity: Current 110V: take flat plugs (adapter required).

Tree-Lighting – *Dec.* Christmas lights, especially at Rockefeller Center and on the corner of 5th Avenue and 59th Street, near Central Park.

For more information, visit the tourist office website: www.nycvisit.com.

GETTING TO NEW YORK

By air

John F. Kennedy International Airport (JFK) – www.airport-jfk.com. To reach New York, the **Air Train** ($7.50) will connect you to the **subway system** ($2.75 ticket). Other solutions: **NY Airport Service bus** (1h-1h30, $16); **shuttles** - Super Shuttle or Go Airlink New York (1 hour, about $19). By **taxi** allow $52 (with tolls) then add a 15-20% tip.

Newark Liberty International Airport (EWR) – www.panynj.gov/airports/newark-liberty.html. To reach New York, the **Air Train** takes you to the **Amtrak network** and the New Jersey Transit ($12.50 total). Other solutions: **NY Airport Service bus** (1h-1h30, $16); **shuttles**: Go Airlink Super Shuttle or New York (1 hour, about $19). By **taxi**, expect $50-75 (and add 15-20% as a tip).

LaGuardia Airport (LGA) – www. panynj.gov/airports/laguardia.html. To reach New York: the **M60 bus** transfers to the subway stations on the lines N and W. Other solutions: **shuttles**: Super Shuttle and Go Airlink New York (45 minutes, about $19). By **taxi**, expect $45 (to which add tolls and a tip).

By sea

From the port of **Southampton** (England), Queen Mary 2 sails to New York in six days (about £2,000). Contact **Cunard** (www.cunard.co.uk) for further information.

WHERE TO STAY

Prepare to spend the bulk of your budget on accommodation.

City guide sites (www.citysearch.com) and New York Net Guide (www.newyorknetguide.com) provide general information on accommodation in New York. The sites below help you find a home, according to your needs and your budget.

Hotels - Overall, the rooms are expensive and small, except in luxury hotels. Many offer only shared bathrooms. There are featured hotels on www.viamichelin.fr or on www.booking.com.

Bed & Breakfast - They are not really cheaper than hotels, but in principle allow guests to meet and discover life in New York. Reservations on: www.bbonline.com, www.bedandbreakfast.com.

Hostels - YMCA (www.ymcanyc.org); Hostelling International (www.hinewyork.org).

Apartment rental - An ideal formula if you stay over a weekend. Reservations on: www.nyhabitat.com; http://newyorkcity.sublet.com; www.new-york-apartment.com; www.airbnb.com.

Tourist information

Online:

www.nycvisit.com (New York tourist office); **www.nyc.gov** (New York city website).

On location:

Official NYC Information Center - Midtown – 810, 7th Ave. - Ⓜ 7th Ave. - ☎ 212 484 1222 - www.nycgo.com.

Official NYC Visitor Center – Times Square Alliance, 1560 Broadway, 7th Ave. - ☎ 212 730 7555.

Hudson Street, Greenwich Village

© Jon Arnold/hemis.fr

LAY OF THE LAND

Manhattan's streets are laid out in a grid pattern. Streets run east–west and avenues run north–south; knowing this helps keep you oriented. Moreover, avenues tend to be wider than streets – you'll be glad to know this when you come up out of a subway wondering which way to turn.

Fifth Avenue is the dividing line between east and west addresses. Though Avenue of the Americas is the official name, New Yorkers prefer to call it by its original name, Sixth Avenue.

Generally, even-numbered streets are eastbound; odd-numbered streets are westbound. In Lower Manhattan (below 14th St.) most streets have names rather than numbers. North of Houston (HOW-stun) Street (with the exception of Greenwich Village), blocks are generally short and wide.

Macy's, Sixth Avenue

© Anton J Geisser/age fotostock

EVENTS

Programming - New York Magazine, Time Out New York and The Village Voice offer comprehensive music, theater and movie listings. Detailed information about what is on in New York is listed on www.nyc.com – you can't go wrong.

Booking - Ticket sales on www.gotickets.com, www.tickco.com, www.ticketmaster.com.

Venues - Enhance your stay by going to a Broadway musical (🎫 *Section 4*). Check for details: www.livebroadway.com. Reduced tickets to the TKTS booths (🎫 *Tips*). Upper West Side is a must for quality concert halls such as Lincoln Center (🎫 *Section 7*). In the North, Harlem is the home of jazz and blues (🎫 *Section 9*).

TELEPHONE AND INTERNET

Calling from New York to Europe - 🖉 011 + country code (44 for UK) + number of your correspondent (without the 0 for the UK).

Calling from New York to New York - Enter the code directly followed by the 7-digit phone number.

WiFi - Many public places, coffee shops and bars have free WiFi; you may have to ask at the counter for the network password. All subway stations provide WiFi service underground.

All public libraries offer free, but unsecured, wireless access in public areas whenever the library is open, and about 20 public parks (check out *www.nycgo.com* for a map of WiFi locations) provide free WiFi hotspots so you won't lose service when you're enjoying the beauty of the city's parks.

SENDING A POSTCARD

Stamps are on sale in post offices, some supermarkets, drugstores or minimarkets. Most hotels in the city are happy to mail your postcards home to family and friends.

Post offices are open from 8h30 to 17h-18h and on Saturday morning. The Central Post Office (441, 8th Ave.) stays open 24/24.

Editorial Director: Cynthia Ochterbeck
Editorial: Sophie Friedman
Contributing Writers: Terry Marsh, Dave Zuckerman, Anna Crine, Matilde Miñon-Marqua, María Guttiérez-Alonso, Guylaine Idoux, Hervé Kerros, Sarah Larrue, Sarah Parot, Pierre Plantier
Cartography: Laurence Sénéchal, Daniel Duguay, Peter Wrenn
Cover & Interior Design: Laurent Muller
Additional Layout: Natasha George
Photo research: Yoshimi Kanazawa, Marie Simonet, Maria Gaspar

Special Sales: travel.lifestyle@us.michelin.com
Contact us: Michelin Travel & Lifestyle North America, One Parkway South, Greenville, SC 29615, USA
travel.lifestyle@us.michelin.com
www.us.michelin.com

Michelin Travel Partner, Hannay House, 39 Clarendon Road, Watford, Herts WD17 1JA, UK
travelpubsales@uk.michelin.com
www.ViaMichelin.com

Printed: September 2017

While every effort is made to ensure that all information printed in this guide is correct and up-to-date, Michelin Travel Partner accepts no liability for any direct, indirect or consequential losses howsoever caused so far as such can be excluded by law. Admission prices listed are for a single adult, unless otherwise specified.

Mapping: © MICHELIN et © 2013-2014 TomTom. All rights reserved. This material is proprietary and the subject of copyright protection, database right protection and other intellectual property rights owned by TomTom or its suppliers. The use of this material is subject to the terms of a license agreement. Any unauthorized copying or disclosure of this material will lead to criminal and civil liabilities.

Weights and measures

1 mile: 1.61 km
69 Fahrenheit: 20° Celsius
Size 6-8 (clothes) = size 10 in UK
Shoe size: womens 8 = 6, mens 8-7.5 in the UK

Museums - The price of admission is often prohibitive, but almost all museums provide free slots or reduced prices at certain times of the week. The **City Pass** and **New York Pass** offer entries to a selection of museums and tourist sites for a fixed price. City Pass: valid for nine days ($109) - www.citypass.com. New York Pass: valid for 1 day ($85), two days ($130), three days ($180) or seven days ($230) - www.newyorkpass.com.

Going out - The TKTS booth in Times Square (*47th St. West*), South Street Seaport (*corner of Front St. and John St.*) and Broadway Downtown (*1 MetroTech Center*) offer unsold tickets, from 25 to 50% cheaper for musicals of the day or the following morning.

Festivals - Shakespeare in the Park, Central Park (June-August), gives free access to live theater (tickets distributed on the same day or at the Delacorte Theater - www.shakespeareinthepark.org).

In summer, in **Bryant Park** (www.bryantpark.org/calendar) **outdoor movies** are projected on Monday nights in the HBO Summer Film Screenings, while **Broadway in Bryant Park** puts on great musicals on Thursday at 12h30.

The **Harlem Meer Performance Festival** program on Sunday afternoon are a series of concerts (jazz, blues, gospel, Latin music) in the northern part of Central Park.

HOURS AND PUBLIC HOLIDAYS

Stores - Monday-Saturday 10h-20h, Thursday 21h.

Museums - They are closed on Mondays and major holidays (Jan. 1, Thanksgiving and Dec 25).

Public holidays - January 1 (New Year's Day); Third Monday of January (Martin Luther King Jr's Birthday); third Monday in February (Presidents' Day); last Monday in May (Memorial Day); July 4 (Independence Day); 1st Monday in September (Labor Day); 2nd Monday of October (Columbus Day); November 11 (Veterans Day); 4th Thursday of November (Thanksgiving Day); December 25 (Christmas Day).

When in New York

Breakfast is taken from 7h and a light lunch is often taken from 11h30. In the summer, many people picnic in the parks.

Dinner is served until 23h, and remains the main meal of the day. The weekend brunch serves as breakfast and lunch combined (between 10h and 16h).

WHERE TO EAT

Specialties - In New York, there is the cuisine of the northeast coast, with specialties of fish and shellfish, such as clam chowder or crab cakes.

Other specialties of tradition are the southern states and Cajun cuisine, with jambalaya (rice with ham and shrimp) or fried and crispy chicken.

Texmex cuisine mixes Mexican influences, Spanish and Texan. Grilled meat Texan-style (barbecued), marinated or not, with or without sauce is a must.

The large Jewish immigration influences a very typical way of eating, notably the famous delicatessen, which mix German, Austrian and Polish influences.

Chelsea Market

INDEX

No. of section ←⎯⎯⎯⎯⎯⎯⎯⎯⎯⎯⎯ L: map page left
Empire State Building .... **6 R** ⎯→ R: map page right

MICHELIN

Michelin Travel Partner

Société par actions simplifiée au capital de 11 288 880 EUR
27 cours de l'Ile Seguin - 92100 Boulogne Billancourt (France)
R.C.S. Nanterre 433 677 721

No part of this publication may be reproduced in any form
without the prior permission of the publisher.

© Michelin Travel Partner
Printer: SOLER (Spain)
Printed in Spain: 10-2017 ISO 14001